www.lanternsofliberty.us

www.lanternsofliberty.us

Washington We are Watching

LANTERNS OF LIBERTY

www.lanternsofliberty.us

Illuminating the Truth
Educational Curriculum

Common Sense
Washington Package

Chris Pilie
Trey Roberts

Lanterns of Liberty Productions

New Orleans Gretna Prairieville, Louisiana

www.lanternsofliberty.us

Lanterns of Liberty
Lanternsofliberty.us

New Orleans, Louisiana

Copyright © 2010 by Christopher M. Pilie

All rights reserved, including the rights to reproduce this Book or portions thereof un any form whatsoever.

For information about this publication contact Lanterns of Liberty at www.lanternsofliberty.us.

Special Thanks to our dear and respected American Patriots

Edited by Chris Pilie
Scott StGermain – Lanterns of Liberty

"America is like a healthy body and its resistance is threefold: its patriotism, its morality, and its spiritual life. If we can undermine these three areas, America will collapse from within."

Josef Stalin

Introduction 10
The Plan – Common Sense 15
Step #1 – Educate - Shock and Awe 18
  Agenda: The Grinding Down of America 19
Step #2 – Inject the Truth – Equalize 22
  The Bloody History of Communism 22
  3. Frankfurt School – Political Correctness 26
  The Weather Underground Documentary 29
  Bresmenov's Communist Subversion Techniques 31
Step #3 – Pull out the thorn – Eradicate 33
  The Mission 33

Introduction

The purpose of this manual is to provide a guideline to educate about the Progression of Secular Socialism and the history of its inevitable goal – communism. The United States has gradually and incrementally become transformed into a more socialist society as its prosperity has brought much apathy to its citizens. In the midst of one of the most historical White House administrations, the American people have awakened to an unexpected vantage point – the fundamental transformation of America.

In order to understand what end our country is destined to achieve, we must understand where we are now and where we have been. When an American President has been quoted saying…

"If you look at the victories and failures of the civil rights movement, and its litigation strategy in the court, I think where it succeeded was to vest formal rights in previously dispossessed peoples, so that I would now have the right to vote, I would now be able to sit at a lunch counter and order and as long as I could pay for it I'd be okay."

"But," Obama said, *"The Supreme Court never ventured into the issues of redistribution of wealth and sort of more basic issues of political and economic justice in this society. And to that extent as radical as I think people tried to characterize the Warren Court, it wasn't that radical. It didn't break free from the essential constraints that were placed by the founding fathers in the Constitution, as least as it's been interpreted, and Warren Court interpreted in the same way that generally the Constitution is a charter of negative liberties, says what the states can't do to you, says what the federal government can't do to you, but it doesn't say what the federal government or the state government must do on your behalf. And that hasn't shifted."*

Obama said "one of the, I think, the tragedies of the civil rights movement, was because the civil rights movement became so court focused, I think that there was a tendency to lose track of the political and community organizing activities on the ground that are able to put together the actual coalitions of power through which you bring about redistributive change, and in some ways we still suffer from that." **Obama on NPR 2001**

…there is much to fear.

This manual is a comprehensive but simple explanation of how to deliver the history of the 20th century and all of its revolution.

www.lanternsofliberty.us

The Plan – Common Sense

This curriculum represents the free speech principles that America was founded on. Thomas Payne was the most famous pamphleteer during the American Revolution and possibly in history. During this time, Thomas Payne wrote "Common Sense" in order to motivate the people to begin considering independence. It was considered to even be treasonous against the British Government.

Obviously this book is not treasonous against the United States government. It is intended to educate, equalize, and eradicate.

1. Educate – Educate your friends, family, neighbors, teachers, pastors, and priests about where our country is in relation to the founding of the country.

2. Equalize - Equalize as many people as possible about the American truth and the Marxist lie. Expose political media bias. The truth is the common thread through all things. Marxists have entered the country many years ago to progress the country away from the truth and towards the lie. To equalize is to help balance all common sense firmly on the truth.

3. Eradicate – Eradication of the ideology of Marxism will take much time. This is done through the previous two steps. We must be missionaries of truth and missionaries of the American Constitution.

The following steps will help you do these three things. You must get the healing truth injected into American societal bloodstream. America is thirsting for the truth and it is your job to quench this thirst. America has a deep festering sore. This sore is the symptom of a thorn that has been shoved into our once great culture. This thorn is Marxism. In order to Educate, Equalize and Eradicate, we must surgically remove the thorn of Marxism and sanitize with the truth. Gather all those willing to listen and explain where we are in these dark but promising days.

The hard to swallow pill is that America is no longer the America that our founders had engineered. Our Constitution has become porous rather than impenetrable. We have become anesthetized by everything that is political, social, and spiritual. We need to withdraw from the matrix of sensationalized entertainment. We need to turn off our television and pick up a book. The great second President of the United States and founding father John Adams once said:

"The science of government it is my duty to study, more than all other sciences; the arts of legislation and administration and negotiation ought to take the place of, indeed exclude, in a manner, all other arts. I must study politics and war, that our sons may have liberty to study mathematics and philosophy. Our sons ought to study mathematics and philosophy, geography, natural history and naval architecture, navigation, commerce and agriculture in order to give their children a right to study painting, poetry, music, architecture, statuary, tapestry and porcelain."

We have come to a time where we owe it to our children and grandchildren to reverse the direction we are headed. Ask yourself if what we are facing is sustainable. Ask if our government is sustainable with its current course. It is our duty to study the science of government so our children can study mathematics and philosophy in good schools so that our grand children can once again study honorable painting, poetry, music, architecture, statuary, tapestry and porcelain that hasn't been perverted by radicalism.

In order to wake up your friends, family, neighbors, teachers, pastors, and priests you must use shock and awe.

www.lanternsofliberty.us

Step #1 – Educate - Shock and Awe

America is on the verge of a fundamental collapse into a communist state. The promises of Khrushchev have been realized. In a dialogue between great conservative Ezra Benson, who was the Secretary of Agriculture under Dwight Eisenhower, and Nikita Khrushchev the truth was revealed concerning the agenda of the Soviet Union and communism.

"Your children will live under communism." Khrushchev said. *"On the contrary,"* Secretary Benson replied, *"My grandchildren will live in freedom as I hope that all people will."* Khrushchev then retorted: *"You Americans are so gullible. No, you won't accept Communism outright; but we'll keep feeding you small doses of Socialism until you will finally wake up and find that you already have Communism. We won't have to fight you; we'll so weaken your economy, until you fall like overripe fruit into our hands."*

We all must understand that the goal of communism is to encompass the earth because of its insatiable desire for domination, power and control over all human-kind. The evils of communism are hard for the average American to comprehend since America has never been ruled under extreme tyranny. In order to deliver this message to the average American, we must hit them with hard facts, a clear perspective of history, and where we exist in the plan of the communist.

Agenda: The Grinding Down of America

Time: *1 hour and 40 minutes*
Place:
- *1-10 people – living room*
- *11-20 – conference room*
- *21-50 – local hall*

Day: *preferable on weekend*
Preparation: *Be sure to read The 5000 Year Leap*

This documentary is a great introduction that will deliver the shock and awe needed to shake the viewer out of apathy. This documentary does have a Christian angle. It must be understood that the number one goal of the communist is to get the people to worship communism rather than worship God. People of faith and especially bind faith are submissive to the laws of God. The communist wishes to co-op this natural attribute of man and persuade him to worship an imperfectable dictorial leader.

When introducing the message of communism in America, you must demand the dialogue 40 minutes into the initial showing of the DVD. Inform the viewers that the first half of the video is going to 40 minutes long so they can use the restroom and get a cup of coffee. Try to refrain from serving sugary snacks because sugar crashes are a bummer.

www.lanternsofliberty.us

1. Encourage everyone to get comfortable
2. Serve coffee
3. Start DVD
- **Play Session 1: Act 1-4 Time [21:10]**
- *Question: Is Communism Dead?*
- *Question: What so bad about Communism?*
- **Play Session 2: Act 5 Time [20:23]**
- *Question: So who started all of this?*
- **Play Session 3: Act 6-7 Time [28:22]**
- *Question: Why are they so against morality?*
- *Question: How have they pulled this off?*
- **Play Session 4: Act 8-9 Time [21:44]**
4. *Question: Have they been successful?*
5. *Question: Is it too late?*
6. *Question: What must be done?*
7. Server water, coffee, and snacks
8. Allow the people watching to discuss freely
9. Your viewers must be comfortable, so encourage them to stretch and use the restroom if they need to.
10. Ask the viewers, "What do you think?"
11. Ask the viewers if they have any questions
12. Restart the DVD
13. Allow viewers to ask questions after the video
14. Schedule the next video viewing
15. Present booklist to the viewers before they leave with your contact information.
16. Start a network by getting emails so you can contact all of your viewers about upcoming events.
17. Encourage the viewers to pick up at least one of the books and so they can discuss it at the next meeting

Recommended reading:

The 5000 Year Leap

This book could be one of the greatest books about America of our day. It explains how far the world has come after 5000 years of tyranny. Once liberty was released through the American Revolution, the ingenuity and greatness of man was released to advance humanity further in from 1776 to current day 10 fold in comparison of the 5000 years prior. This book is a pre-requisite to knowing the truth about America.

The United States Constitution
The Declaration of Independence

Recommended audio: CD 1

1. Ezra Benson – The Warning
2. Ezra Benson – The Constitution
3. Marion Romney – Socialism and the United Order

Step #2 – Inject the Truth – Equalize

The Bloody History of Communism

Time: *2 Hours*
Place:
- *1-10 people – living room*
- *11-20 – conference room*
- *21-50 – local hall*

Day: *preferable on weekend*
Preparation: *Be sure to read The Machine: The Progression of Secular Socialism*

This DVD is very long and intense. It must be delivered correctly or your viewers could get fatigued. Although the video is long, it is very important. In order to keep the video effective, there needs to be interactive engagement with the viewers. It is important to start the video sharply in order to maintain the viewer's urgency for discussion. Inform the viewers that the first half of the video is going to 1 hour long so they can use the restroom and get a cup of coffee. Try to refrain from serving sugary snacks because sugar crashes are a bummer.

1. Encourage everyone to get comfortable
2. Serve coffee
3. Start DVD

www.lanternsofliberty.us

4. After about 1 hour, stop the DVD for a break
5. Server water, coffee, and snacks (not sugary)
6. Allow the people watching to discuss freely
7. Your viewers must be comfortable, so encourage them to stretch and use the restroom if they need to.
8. Ask the viewers, "What do you think?"
9. Ask the viewers if they have any questions
10. Restart the DVD
11. Allow viewers to ask questions after the video
12. Schedule the next video viewing
13. Present booklist to the viewers before they leave with your contact information.

Encourage the viewers to pick up at least one of the books and so they can discuss it at the next meeting

Recommended reading:

The Machine: The Progression of Secular Socialism
Purchase at **www.LanternsOfLiberty.us**

The Machine: Progression of Secular Socialism is a book that marries well with both the *Agenda* DVD and *The Bloody History of Communism* documentary. It peers into the history of Progressivism and its gradualist and incremental influence on destroying the culture and prosperity of America.

Recommended Audio: CD 2

1. **The Communist Manifesto**
2. **Ronald Reagan – Socialize Medicine**
3. **Ronald Reagan – Goldwater Speech**

www.lanternsofliberty.us

Frankfurt School – Political Correctness

Time: *30 minutes*
Place:
- *1-10 people – living room*
- *11-20 – conference room*
- *21-50 – local hall*

Day: *preferable on weekend*
Preparation: *Be sure to read The Machine: The Progression of Secular Socialism*

This video is extremely important. It outlines the introduction of Marxism. This video is only 30 minutes ling so some deep discussion needs to occur. By this time the viewers are ready to discuss. This where the viewers need to have their newly discovered knowledge exposed to the group. Encourage the viewers that their knowledge is welcome and important. Be sure to correct them if their logic is out of step with the truth. It is imperative to ask some specific question.

1. Encourage everyone to get comfortable
2. Serve coffee
3. Start DVD
4. Allow viewers to ask questions after the video

- Question 1: How has Marxism entered the United States?

- Question 4: What is the difference between the conventional education system different then the Progressive education system.
- Question 3: How has the Progressive education system change America?

5. Schedule the next video viewing
6. Present booklist to the viewers before they leave with your contact information.

Recommended Reading:

Rules for Radicals by Saul Alinsky

Having influenced people like Barack Obama and Hillary Clinton and much of the community organizing activists, Saul Alinsky must be realized as the American Marxist. In order to truly understand the Progressive agenda, one must understand the "any means to the desired end" philosophy. Saul Alinsky proposes that no ethics and morals can progress a society. The means to get to the end need to be separated from morals and ethics. Learn the hand book of political principles of the uber-left.

Recommended Audio: CD 3

1. **Ezra Benson – The Race Against Time**
2. **George Bernard Shaw – Mussolini Stance**
3. **George Bernard Shaw – Humane Gas**

www.lanternsofliberty.us

4. **George Bernard Shaw - Constitution**

The Weather Underground Documentary

Time: 92 minutes
Place:
- 1-10 people – living room
- 11-20 – conference room
- 21-50 – local hall

Day: preferable on weekend
Preparation: Be sure to read The Machine: The Progression of Secular Socialism

This documentary shows the true colors of the inroads to communism in America. SDS turned Weatherman Bill Ayers and Bernadine Dohrn led the leftist terrorists to bomb and pillage American cities. The documentary exposes the extreme revolutionary, anti-colonialism, and communist sympathizing degenerates that have failed to overthrow America. Although they have failed, they have not disappeared. Currently, Bill Ayers along with his other Weatherman have been involved in writing public policy, receiving tax dollars to fund radical left wing front groups, and are involved in Marxist education in our collegiate education system.

1. Encourage everyone to get comfortable
2. Serve coffee
3. Start DVD
4. After about 40 minutes, stop the DVD for a break

www.lanternsofliberty.us

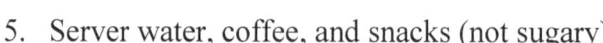

5. Server water, coffee, and snacks (not sugary)
6. Allow the people watching to discuss freely
7. Your viewers must be comfortable, so encourage them to stretch and use the restroom if they need to.
8. Ask the viewers, "What do you think?"
9. Ask the viewers if they have any questions
10. Restart the DVD
11. Detail what involvement these individuals have in the political and social environment. (Use The Machine and your own research)
12. Allow viewers to ask questions after the video
13. Schedule the next video viewing
14. Present booklist to the viewers before they leave with your contact information.

Recommended Reading:

The Coming Insurrection by the Invisible Committee

This book is the declaration of the communist. This book surfaced in France and has made world wide impact as a manifesto of the communists and pseudo-anarchists. This book will scare the pants off of the average American that is grounded in capitalism and principles of the family. The book seems to prophesize the destruction of the world's capitalist nature and brings about a new utopia.

www.lanternsofliberty.us

Bresmenov's Communist Subversion Techniques

Time: 1 Hour and 3 minutes
Place:
- *1-10 people – living room*
- *11-20 – conference room*
- *21-50 – local hall*

Day: preferable on weekend
Preparation: Be sure to read The Machine: The Progression of Secular Socialism

Former Soviet KGB operative Yuri Bresmenov's communist subversion technique education is legendary. Yuri's light humor mixed with his heavy Russian accent is very convincing. His first hand knowledge of the communist system and the subversive techniques of taking over a country and converting it to a Communist regime is fundamental in understanding what has happened to America.

1. Encourage everyone to get comfortable
2. Serve coffee
3. Start DVD
4. Allow the people watching to discuss freely
5. Ask your viewers for examples of the techniques and how they have been used in America
6. Allow viewers to ask questions after the video

www.lanternsofliberty.us

7. Schedule the next video viewing
8. Present booklist to the viewers before they leave with your contact information.

Recommended Reading:

Liberty and Tyranny by Mark Levin

Mark Levin is most known for his talk radio show where he relentlessly exposes the radical leftist agenda and idiocy of its illogical ideology. Liberty and Tyranny has become the manifesto of the Tea Party movement. The books explains the march of tyranny and the existence of a "soft tyranny" which Alexis-Charles-Henri Clérel de Tocqueville coined in his 1835 work *Democracy in America*. This book will expose the radical left agenda and the illogical sense behind it.

Step #3 – Pull out the thorn – Eradicate

The Mission

Now is the time to get those that you have educated to now educate. Encourage those that you educated to spread the word of truth about where our country is. There are many ways to deliver this message. You can have those that you have educated to bring you others that need to be educated or you can mentor those that you have educated to educate others.

Lanterns of Liberty is a hub to this cause. Sign up for free on LanternsOfLiberty.us for further releases and education material. The site has a weekly newsletter that will keep you informed on all the latest news, issues, and events. Lanterns of Liberty is continuously releasing educational material along with books to giver perspective during this pivotal time in our country's history.

www.ingramcontent.com/pod-product-compliance
Lightning Source LLC
Chambersburg PA
CBHW031439040426
42444CB00006B/891